In God's Image

Published by the C. R. Gibson Company, Norwalk, CT 06856

Printed in the U.S.A.

ISBN 0-8378-1817-6

GB 703

In God's Image

Meditations For The New Mother

by
Patricia Houck Sprinkle

The C. R. Gibson Company
Norwalk, CT 06856

Dedicated to Barnabas and David—who
daily grow in the image of God.

Foreword

When I had my first baby, I looked forward to teaching my child about God. I never imagined that in their first year, babies teach us far more about God than we teach them!

I did not realize that when God creates a person in His image, He does so from the very beginning. We who yearn to know God better can learn much about Him from those He has recently stamped with His likeness.

Even before my babies were born, I found that thoughts of the baby were often linked with thoughts of God. During the year after each birth, I discovered that God used my baby to teach me not only about my role as a parent, but about my role as a child of God, and a member of God's whole family.

My prayer for each one who reads this book is that you and *your* baby will also share in the special joys that come as you teach each other about what it means to be members of God's family.

Patricia Houck Sprinkle

Before I formed you in the womb I knew
you.   Jeremiah 1:5

Waiting

I wish you'd come, Little One. As I move ponderously about
the house or wedge myself between supermarket displays,
I am heavy with longing for you to be born. I am so eager to
see you, hold you, discover just exactly who and what you
are. Are you a girl or a boy? Do you have your daddy's hair,
or my nose? Hurry, Baby! When you get here, you'll have a
lot more room than you do now for kicks and stretches. We'll
cuddle and play, have such fun together.

But you are content to slumber where you are. Are you
afraid to risk a new environment? Come on, Baby! It's not
much of a risk. I'll be here, after all.

And as I wait, impatient with longing, I wonder: Is this
how God feels, waiting for us to find Him or for us to come
back to Him when we have drifted away? Does God, too,
yearn to stir my spirit as I struggle with my doubts and fears
until I take that one final step of faith and say, "Hello. Here
I am. I believe!"? How can God stand the waiting?

In the beginning was the Word...The
Word became flesh and lived for a while
among us.   John 1:1, 14

Newborn

Welcome to our family,
Beloved One!
   Most of today I spent holding you, curled into a ball, on my
chest, cradled your grapefruit head
against my chin. Now you lie on your
tummy in your bassinet beside my bed.
As you lift your tiny rear, give a lurch, and slide one knee
across the sheet, I gasp in comprehension. *That's* what you
were doing these past few days!

   As I gently stroke your back, I marvel. Yesterday you were
only a word: Baby. Only a ripple within me, a dream, a hope.
Now today you are YOU: someone with a name, a face, a
personality of your very own. Yesterday you were someone I
could talk about. Today you are someone I can talk *to*. A Bible
phrase comes to my mind: "the word became flesh."

   By being born, you help me understand your former mystery, your reality. Isn't that what Jesus did? He made the
nebulous word "God" into a person—someone with a name,
a personality. You become very holy to me, Child, when I
realize that when God wanted to show exactly what He was
like, He sent a baby.

This is the day the Lord has made; let us
rejoice and be glad in it.   Psalms 118:24

One Day Old

Before you came, I knew that I would love you. I knew that
there was room in my heart for you. But I thought that it
would take time for us to bond. That my love for you would
grow a little each day. After all, that's how love is supposed
to happen.

What a surprise! They brought you to me for the very first
time. As I held you and looked into the haze of your new-
born eyes, I knew that I had been wrong. My love for you
was complete. So overwhelming that I'm afraid to let you go,
even to the arms of Nurse.

I grow anxious at the thought of losing you. My imagina-
tion works overtime. Will I drift off to sleep and let you fall?
Are you really breathing?

God alone knows how far we will travel together on earth,
Little One. Today I am aware of how fragile you are, and
I cherish every hour, every minute we have together.

*In my Father's house are many rooms;
...I am going there to prepare a place
for you.*   John 14:2

Three Days Old

Well, Little One, it is time to go home.

I assemble your clothes and begin to change you from your hospital shirt and diaper into new ones. These are your very own, Child—the others were merely borrowed. But those borrowed ones are the only ones you've ever known, and so, as I try to dress you, you protest mightily. When I move about the room packing up, you screw up your face and cry lustily. Don't you want to go home?

We've prepared a very special place for you—a crib of your own, a chest full of clothes, a basket of toys and books. There are warm blankets there, and a colorful mobile to swing above your crib.

I know this room is all you've known, that you've been here your whole lifetime. I understand that it is hard to leave. But trust me, Little One. There is a big, beautiful world out there.

Jesus said, "I go to prepare a place for you." Jesus was talking about dying. But He could have been talking about change—any change. Maybe He was saying to me what I'm saying to you. "Cheer up, Child. I've already been there, getting things ready. Come with me to a big, new life!"

And you will receive the gift of the Holy Spirit. Acts 2:38

One Week Old

Lying very close to you, my chin nestled on your fuzzy crown, I almost wonder if you're still alive, Little One. You are so deep in sleep that you do not move.

But then I feel your warm breath on my throat. Each puff reassures me that you are strong, vital, alive.

Isn't it interesting that the Hebrew word for "spirit"—*ruach*—also means breath? The breath of God moved across the waters in creation. The breath of God blew like a whirlwind at Pentecost. The breath of God comes into our lives and stirs us with power and love.

Each puff of the Holy Spirit reassures us that God is strong, vital, alive!

*Greater love has no one than this, that
one lay down his life for his friends.*
John 15:13

Ten Days Old

Who could have imagined that a tiny baby could take up so much time? For three days I have planned to get to the store for potting soil and pots to transplant the geraniums. But day after day, I find that I hardly have time for a shower—all my time is full of you.

I pick up the laundry, then lay it down to change you. I gather dirty dishes, then lay them down to feed you. I pick up my car keys, but lay them down because you've already started your nap. Jesus said we are to lay down our lives for other people. Is this what He meant? Does laying down my life mean laying down the laundry, the dishes, the novel I'd saved to read until after you were born?

Society tells me to do my own thing, to meet my own needs. These are worthwhile goals, but Jesus points me to a greater good. A love that recognizes my own needs and deliberately, joyfully puts them aside for someone else. It looks like you, Little One, have come to help me learn that kind of love!

Ask, and it will be given to you.
Matthew 7:7

Two Weeks Old

I'm coming, Child.
I was sitting in my room having a time of prayer when I heard your first little whimper, and I knew you were hungry. Since that first cry, I've been getting ready to feed you, assuring you softly that you are going to eat soon. But still you cry louder and louder. As we settle into our rocker, you are screaming with rage.

Hush, Little One. Do you really think I will refuse you what you need? Don't you know yet how much I love you?

Now, while you nurse, I will get back to the prayer I left when you began to cry. Where was I? Oh, yes. I was reminding God again that I need...

What's that? I thought I heard Someone whisper, "I heard you the first time, too. Don't you know how much I love YOU?"

*I am the Alpha and the Omega, the First
and the Last, the Beginning and the End.*
Revelation 22:13

Seventeen Days Old

Sometimes, some very special times, as I sit rocking you in
dimness, time seems to part gently like a dimple on a pool's
surface. Together we sink into a marvelous gift of
timelessness.

The Greeks have a word for it: *kairos*. That means "the
strategic time," or "God's time." A time that has no beginning
and no end.

As your tiny head melts into the curve of my arm and our
bodies fuse in warmth, I lose all sense of time passing by.

It is not that time stands still, but rather that we no longer
stand within time. We become a part of time itself.

Thank you, Small One, for leading me to the threshhold of eternity.

I urge you to live a life worthy of the call-
ing you have received.   Ephesians 4:1

Three Weeks Old

What do you see, Little One, as your eyes focus far beyond
my shoulder while I bend over your crib? What do you hear?
What do you think about, so intent on something I cannot
see?

Today, for the first time, I realize that you and I are separate, and the thought makes me a little afraid. I know, of
course, that you have been a separate person for a long time,
even when you were cradled within me, but I have grown so
accustomed to thinking of you as a part of me. Today I realize
that one day you will grow up—and away.

As you grow, you will see, hear, and believe things that are
not what I see, hear, or believe. You may like things that I dislike, and dislike some things that I love. God and you together may even choose for you a purpose, a path, that is not
at all what I would have chosen for you.

Don't hurry, Child. I know that it will nòt be easy to let you
go. I need time to pray that God will give me grace not only
to bear, but also to encourage your growth toward independence. I will pray too, Little One, that whatever path you
take, you will walk with God.

Be still, and know that I am God.
Psalms 46:10

Four Weeks Old

We both learned an important lesson today, Little One.

It was a busy day, with lots of company and a hectic schedule. My "superwoman" complex kept me rushing here and there, and when you got hungry I fed you almost without thinking, continuing my conversations and expecting you to hurry to meet my schedule.

But you weren't willing to hurry. You whined and fretted, growing tense and anxious.

Then a wise friend suggested we go off into a quiet room, just you and me. We rocked and shared a smile. (You did smile, didn't you?) And in peace, you nursed contentedly.

Once again God was teaching me through you. Like you, God doesn't want to be squeezed into the corners of my busy-ness. Like you, I get my best feedings in quiet, private moments of total communion.

Why do I expose you to hectic feedings and myself to hectic prayers when I know the best nourishment is available in quiet corners?

I am the good shepherd; I know my sheep
and my sheep know me.   John 10:14

Five Weeks Old

How special, Beloved. You are beginning to know me! Even
in a room full of people, you turn your head toward my
voice. How your face lights up when I speak! Soon, the ex-
perts tell me, you will even pick my face from a crowd, but
for now you go only by the voice. When you get anxious, nobody else will do. Only my voice, or sometimes that of your
daddy, can calm you.

Watching you strain to listen makes me want to improve
my own listening skills. I want to hear the voice of my Heavenly Parent. To pick Him out from all the others. Like you,
when I need comfort, nobody else will do. Show me by your
example how to tune my ears to the One voice my heart
yearns to hear.

God is our refuge and strength, an ever
present help in trouble. Psalms 46:1

Six Weeks Old

At your first gasp of alarm, I
am alert. Before you begin to
cry, I am on my way to you,
because I know that gasp. It
means you are in trouble you can't handle.

What is it this time? Has your blanket covered your face
again? Did the toy you were holding tumble to the floor? Or,
has the music box wound down again?

Little babies have little troubles, but they are very real.
That's why I hurry to your side. I want you to feel that you
are protected, watched over.

If I delay, I feel Someone within me, nudging me along.
And guess what? As I learn to listen for your sounds of
alarm, my ears are being tuned to hear alarm in others. Is
God using me to be an ever-present help to those in trouble?

This is how you should pray: "Our
Father in heaven..."   Matthew 6:9

Seven Weeks Old

My child, you are so basic. Your relationship to me consists almost entirely of "give me" (food, a blanket), "take it away" (an uncomfortable diaper), "love me" (hold me) and, sometimes, "I love you, too."

You make me think about my relationship to God. I realize how many of my prayers to Him consist only of "give me," "take it away," "love me" and, only sometimes, "I love you, too."

But every day I see that you are learning to give, Child. To hug, to reach out, to coo with delight. I need to learn to give more to God, too. If I am to help you grow up, I need to grow myself.

As we grow together we'll learn to communicate more maturely. But let's not forget that Jesus always began his prayers with the childish *Abba*, "Daddy." God is the Daddy of us all.

Let your gentleness be evident to all.
Philippians 4:5

Eight Weeks Old

Grandmother's car just pulled away, taking you with her. It's the first time you have ever gone anywhere without me, Little One, and I found myself watching her car until it was out of sight.

I should have been planning my free afternoon, but instead I could only think about the accidents that could happen, the worries that might be going on behind your puckered little brow. Again I remember how fragile you are, how easily you could break. When we brought you home from the hospital, how slowly I made your daddy drive! And that first night, how often I got up to be sure that you were still breathing! By now I am used to driving around with you and am accustomed to your almost breathless sleep. But when the car carrying you disappeared, I trembled with fear.

I think it is good for me to remember again how fragile you are, Child. It makes me gentler with you. It also reminds me how fragile all people are, even those who look big and strong. Keep reminding me of how easily people break, Little One, until I learn to be gentle with everyone.

Then God said, "Let us make (human beings) in our image."   Genesis 1:26

Ten Weeks Old

As you lie on your blanket, waving your hands and feet and trying to understand your fingers and toes, you give me such pleasure, Child! You gurgle deep in your throat and then light up with such a wide, toothless grin that I have to grin, too. I touch your cheek, ruffle your fuzzy hair, and I love you so much it makes me shiver.

We adults like to think of ourselves as very "grown up." But guess what, Little One? I suspect that when we are at our most serious—involved in our deepest discussions, proudest of our physical achievements, congratulating ourselves on our latest success—we are actually as amusing to our heavenly Parent as you are to me just now, lying there so intent on catching that sunbeam.

Why did God choose to create people in His own image? We don't know. But I hope that God gets as much pleasure from watching us as I get from watching you.

Do not let your hearts be troubled. Trust
in God, trust also in me.   John 14:1

Three Months Old

Tonight was dark and stormy,
and we had to attend a large
meeting. You did your best to
smile at the strangers, but finally you began to fret. You were
tired, and the room was much too bright and noisy.

At last I took you over near the fire and rocked you quietly.
There, surrounded by thunder, lightning and noise, you
turned your cheek to me and fell peacefully asleep.

Adults have times, too, Little One, when the hustle and
bustle of life overwhelm them. We, too, get fretful and anxious. But as I watch you lie with complete abandon in my
lap, sleeping the trusting sleep of infancy amid the chaos, I
remember Jesus asleep in a boat on a storm-tossed sea. I remember that God has promised to keep us safe at all times in
His everlasting arms.

I forget that message too often, my child. Thank you for
reminding me that when life gets stormy and crowded, I,
too, have a safe place on the lap of my heavenly Parent.

I tell you the truth, anyone who will not receive the kingdom of God like a little child will not enter it. Mark 10:15

Four Months Old

This morning as I lifted you from your crib to your swing and dangled your rag doll until you chortled with glee, I wondered if that child could have been as little as you. If so, was Jesus reminding us how dependent we are on our heavenly Parent?

We adults take pride in our independence, our self-sufficiency. But the truth is, Little One, that we can no more move into tomorrow without God than you can move alone from your bed to your swing. We depend more on God for our next breath than you depend on me for your next meal.

The difference between adults and infants is that you don't mind being dependent. You have no hang-ups about asking for and receiving my help. You call me when you need me and reward me for my assistance with grins and giggles.

Sometimes I insist on being independent when I don't feel it, because I hate to ask anyone for help, even God. But I'm not always as independent as I like to pretend. Sometimes I really do need help. Thank you, Child, for showing me there's nothing the matter with asking for help when you need it.

There is...one God and Father of all who
is over all and through all and in all.
Ephesians 4:4-6

Five Months Old

How you stretch my world, Little One!

Just having you in my arms brings strangers to my side,
and we become sisters in the mystery that is motherhood.
One tells me of her hard labor, and we commiserate as we
share stories of pain. Another speaks of her child's ear infec-
tion, and we share worries over our babies' health. A third
shyly says, "What a lovely baby," and joy floods her face as
I reply, "And your little boy is so strong!"

What does it matter that we do not know one another's
name, that we vote differently, that our bank accounts are as
different as our ethnic backgrounds? What matters is that we
have something important in common: our babies.

As I push you home from the park, I think that motherhood is very like the Family of God. Why do I spend so much
time noticing my differences from other Christians? All that
really matters is that we have something important in common: our love for Jesus.

For in him we live, and move, and have
our being.   Acts 17:28

Six Months Old

Poor little baby. You desperately want to crawl, but your arms
and legs won't obey. Every time you lurch toward your red
ball, you find that somehow you have backed farther away
from it instead. How furious you are!

If only I could make you understand that you are doing
fine. Going backwards is your first step in going forwards,
Little One. At least you are now moving. Last week you
couldn't even do that. Don't you see how proud Mama and
Daddy are of you?

No, all you can see is that red ball, moving farther away.
You don't realize that the process you are going through is
much more important than that silly ball.

Watching you makes me wonder how often I am just like
you. I think I am succeeding in my walk of faith, then something happens and I fail. "I'm going backwards," I wail,
furious with myself.

But watching you today, I remember how often I learn
good lessons from my failures. I begin to
wonder. Is it possible that times that look to
me like failures are just another part of God's
faith-growth process?

*That night the Lord appeared to him
and said,"...Do not be afraid, for I am
with you."*   Genesis 26:24

Six-And-One-Half Months Old

Hush, Baby, Mama's right here. I only stepped into the yard
for a few minutes to bring in your clothes from the line.
Lately, every time I am out of sight you get worried. Trust
me, Beloved. I'll be right back.

I wonder if that's why the Bible says so often, "Don't be
afraid." We can't always see what God is doing for us. Sometimes He seems to have disappeared, and we feel so lonely,
so abandoned.

But listen! There's a voice even in dark and lonely times, a
voice that says gently, "Trust me, Beloved. I'll be right back."

Even the very hairs of your head are all numbered.   Matthew 10:30

Seven Months Old

You lie beside me on the bed while I read. You are awake, but you are not yet alert. You give me an adoring smile and stare at me intently, memorizing my face.

"Counting my freckles?" I tease, reaching over to tickle your tummy. You chortle and grab my hair, giving it a gentle tug.

I remember something Jesus said, that God has counted every hair on my head.

When you were looking at me just now, your eyes reflected the very love of God.

*Wash away all my iniquity and cleanse
me from my sin.* Psalms 51:2

Seven-And-One-Half Months Old

Which is grubbier, learning to crawl or learning to eat? Lately,
you seem to need three baths a day!

But how you love those baths—splashing, letting droplets
fall from your fingers, tasting the soap to see if it tastes better
this time. You gurgle and goo and crow with delight as your
yellow duck bobs out of reach.

I love the baths too—washing you and watching your soft
pink skin emerge from the dirt or beets. Wrapping you in a
fluffy towel, playing peek-a-boo, letting you lie bare to the
world enjoying a gentle breeze. It's a good thing that bath
times are so special, Little One, for we seem to have a lot of
them lately.

Watching you in your bath reminds me of the way I feel
after confessing my sins to God—clean, refreshed, and
pounds lighter.

There is a time for everything, and a
season for every activity under heaven.
Ecclesiastes 3:1

Eight Months Old

Today while I prepared to shower, I put you in the playpen with some favorite toys and a brand new book. "Please give me ten minutes?" I asked. "Read your book."

Instead, you stood and clung to the rail, clamoring to be let out. "Silly child, it's only temporary," I called. But still you yelled.

And I've been doing the same thing this week, haven't I? Thinking of the freedom I had before you were born, freedom to meet a friend for lunch or eat pie in a restaurant with your daddy late at night. I have been whining and grumbling about being "stuck" at home with a baby (that's YOU!) When I could have been planting flowers, baking a cake, enjoying you, I've been standing at the screen door looking longingly up the road.

What's the matter with us, Child? Do we fear we'll be trapped in these playpens forever? Why can't we both see how temporary they are—and enjoy for now the playthings we've been given?

I'm coming to get you now. Let's go outside together.

Rejoice with those who rejoice; mourn with those who mourn. Romans 12:15

Eight-And-One-Half Months Old

Some days what I do for you seems so repetitive, so trivial. As I heat jars of baby food, find yet another outfit to replace the third one you've dirtied today, or read your favorite book for the second time in an hour, I wonder if anything I do for you is *really* important.

Then you fall, bump! It isn't much, a tiny cut. But when a drop of blood oozes out, you begin to roar: "Mama, Mama!" Tears streaming down your cheeks, you hold it out for me to see.

Solemnly we apply a dab of antiseptic, a colorful bandage. Then I scoop you up, still hiccupping, and carry you out for a cuddle on the grass.

A yellow and black butterfly lands near us, and your eyes sparkle behind their tears. "Puk, puk," you gurgle.

"Bug," I agree. And we share a hug and a laugh.

Much of what I do for you seems trivial, Little One. But when I am there to share your sorrows and your joys, that's very important indeed!

*At the name of Jesus every knee should
bow...* Philippians 2:10

Nine Months Old

You stand under the kitchen table beside
my knees and roar.

You want to come up onto my lap, but
you bump your head every time you try.
"Bow your head and bend your knees,"
I urge. I put my hand on your head and
try to gently press you down a little.

But you don't want to bow your head nor bend your
knees. So there you stand—unbowed, unbent, unhappy.

I want to hold you, Little One, but there's no way for you
to come up to me unless you bow your head and bend your
knees. What a frustrating situation.

You remind me of myself when I feel separated from God
and know it's because of something I've done, or something
He wants me to do that I'm unwilling to do. I don't want to
bow my head and bend my knees to Him, either.

Why are you so stubborn, I wonder? Can't you see I am
waiting? Suddenly you catch on. Carefully you bend and
bow, take one hesitant step and I catch you before you fall.

Why am I so stubborn, I wonder? My Father is waiting.

Unless you change and become like children, you will never enter the kingdom of heaven.   Matthew 18:3

Nine-And-One-Half Months Old

How delighted you are with yourself! Having mastered a chair, you now want to scale the table. Every day you have to explore each piece of furniture, to see what new abilities you have acquired since yesterday. And you are having such fun.

When did I lose that self-delight? What happened to my awareness that every day I can do some things I have never been able to do before? What made me content to stop trying out yesterday's impossibilities to see if they could be done today?

Does being grown up mean being content with "what is" when we could be striving for "what could be"? Inspire me, Child, to stretch my world as you stretch yours.

We do not know what we ought to pray,
but the Spirit himself intercedes for us
with groans that words cannot express.
Romans 8:26

Ten Months Old

You sure talk a lot, Little One. A strange language spoken
only by babies. Sometimes you are so frustrated by people's
inability to comprehend, that you fall back to a pointing fin-
ger and "uh-uh-uh!"

Don't worry. Most of the time we know what you want.
We know you, you see, so we can translate.

Today I read in Romans that the Holy Spirit does the very
same thing. When my prayers get bogged down in feelings I
just don't know how to express, the Spirit will interpret them
for me.

I guess all loving parents are good translators!

He who finds his life will lose it, and he
who loses his life for my sake will find it.
Matthew 10:39

Ten-And-One-Half Months Old

Silly Baby. You want to play ball, but you don't understand
the rules. I can't catch the ball unless you throw it. So, you sit
there with a bewildered expression. "Why won't she play
with me?" you seem to be thinking.

But I can't play with you as long as you keep the ball. You
have to trust me for a little while, roll the ball to me and
count on me to return it. Then we will have a marvelous
game!

You remind me of myself when I clutch onto people or
things and then wonder why they seem to slip from my
grasp. Jesus pointed out that whatever we try to hold onto
we will lose, that we only get what we are willing to give
away. When I am willing to relax my grasp and give
something to Him, He gives back far more than
I gave.

O.K., Child. Roll the ball, and we'll play a
game!

How great is the love the Father has
lavished on us, that we should be called
children of God!   I John 3:1

Eleven Months Old

Some older boys dropped by to play with you this afternoon,
and in their ten-year-old exuberance they were rough. You
became apprehensive, then frightened. Finally you looked
wildly around and wept. One of the boys reached down and
picked you up. "Cut it out," he told the others. I could have
hugged him.

I had been watching all the time, you see, aching to inter-
fere. How I hate to see you frightened, hurt, or excluded
by other children! But you must learn to live in this often
cruel world, so I stood back for a time—and hurt. Until
you were born, I never knew the intense pain of noninterfer-
ing love.

Now I look with different eyes when I see some of God's
children being frightened, injured, or excluded by others.
I used to think about the children's pain. Now I see with parent's eyes. Now I know a little of what God must suffer, too.

I marvel that He can watch as long as He does without
interfering. How can He bear so much pain?

I know that I need to stand up for God's hurting children
and say, "Cut it out!"

He makes me lie down in green pastures,
he leads me beside still waters.

Psalms 23:2

Eleven-And-One-Half Months Old

What a hectic week! With all this rain, we are both getting the cooped-up grumblies. This morning, while I was cleaning up the sugar you'd dumped on the kitchen floor, you were busily shredding tissues. While I was cleaning up the tissues, you were dusting the bathroom—and yourself—with my good bath powder. If you hadn't looked so cute, I would have cried.

Then a friend called with a proposal that I couldn't refuse. I'll take yours for the afternoon, if you take mine next Thursday. Great, I thought. I'll clean and iron...My friend suggested that I "go smell a few roses instead."

I went to the park and stayed for a concert. But I felt a little guilty, and deep inside I worried a bit—were you all right?

I arrived back to find you busily playing with my friend's little girl. Now we're home, refreshed by our time apart. I need time for myself sometimes, Little One, but I praise God I have you to come home to.

Let everything that breathes praise the
Lord! Praise the Lord!   Psalms 150:6

One Year Old Today!

I watch you in your crib, playing your early morning games, unaware that I am there. Then you look up, see me in the door. Instantly you pull yourself up, bounce up and down in joy, shrieking, "Mama! Mama! Mama!" What a marvelous way to start the day!

Is this what praise is all about? Is it just the natural way we humans react when we suddenly sense the presence of someone we adore? There are times when God seems so near that I want to jump up and down and stretch my arms toward Him crying, "Lord! Lord! Lord!" Praise is love and adoration spontaneously pouring out of us, simply because our Beloved IS.

Does God need our praise? I don't know. But for all that He has been and will be, for all that He has taught me about Himself this past year through you, my child, I praise the Lord!

PRAISE THE LORD!

A Letter To My Child